LEARN ABOUT THE HISTORY OF...

Stone, Bronze, & Iron Ages • La Tène culture • Helvetian & Roman Control • Old Swiss Confederacy • Reformation Era • Ulrich Zwingli & John Calvin • Ursuline Order Swiss Revolution & Federal Statehood • Industrialization & Infrastructure • Gotthard Railway • World Wars 1 & 2 Post War Prosperity • Historical Locations • Roman Aventicum • Chillon Castle • Abbey of St. Gall • Wooden Bridge Chapel • Cathedral of St. Pierre • Historical People William Tell • Jean-Jacques Rousseau • Henri Dunant Albert Einstein • Charles-Édouard Jeanneret • Historical Foods • Fondue • Raclette • Rösti • Zürcher Geschnetzeltes • Swiss • Chocolate • Swiss Alps • Sports • Football • Ice Hockey • Alpine Skiing • Tennis • Cycling

ILLUSTRATED WITH HISTORICAL PHOTOS

STONE, BRONZE, & IRON AGES

Switzerland has a long archaeological history that dates back thousands of years. The country has witnessed significant periods of human development, including the Stone, Bronze, and Iron Ages. The Stone Age, the earliest known period of human history, was characterized by the use of stone tools and weapons. In Switzerland, the Stone Age is divided into three distinct phases: the Paleolithic, Mesolithic, and Neolithic.

During the Paleolithic period, which spanned from approximately 2.5 million to 10,000 BCE, early humans were primarily nomadic hunter-gatherers. They roamed the Swiss landscape, relying on stone tools, such as hand axes and flint blades, to hunt animals and gather food. The Mesolithic period, also known as the Middle Stone Age, lasted from around 10,000 to 5000 BCE. During this time, Switzerland witnessed a gradual shift from a nomadic lifestyle to settled communities. People began to establish semi-permanent settlements near water sources, engaging in fishing, hunting, and gathering activities. The tools of this era became smaller, more specialized, and often made from microliths, tiny stone flakes used for various purposes like arrowheads and scrapers.

The Neolithic period, roughly spanning from 5000 to 2200 BCE, brought about significant changes in Swiss society. The advent of agriculture revolutionized the way people lived. Communities began cultivating crops, such as wheat and barley, and domesticating animals like cattle, sheep, and goats. Farming allowed settlements to grow larger and more permanent. Tools evolved with the introduction of ground and polished stone implements, such as sickles and axes. The construction of megalithic structures, including dolmens and menhirs, also became prominent during this time, indicating a belief in spiritual and ceremonial practices.

The Bronze Age in Switzerland, which lasted from approximately 2200 to 800 BCE, marked a period when bronze, an alloy of copper and tin, replaced stone as the primary material for tools and weapons. This transition had a profound impact on Swiss society, leading to advancements in technology, trade, and social organization. During the Early Bronze Age, Switzerland witnessed the emergence of metalworking and the production of bronze objects. Artisans crafted weapons, such as swords and daggers, as well as jewelry and decorative items. These valuable artifacts were often associated with the elites, reflecting social hierarchies within communities.

With the introduction of bronze, agricultural techniques also improved. Bronze tools, including plows and sickles, allowed for more efficient farming and increased agricultural productivity. The surplus of food led to population growth and the establishment of larger settlements. The Late Bronze Age saw the rise of fortified hilltop settlements, known as hillforts, in Switzerland. These settlements were strategically located and protected by defensive walls, suggesting the need for increased security and protection. Hillforts also functioned as centers of trade, craft production, and social gatherings.

The Iron Age, spanning from approximately 800 to 15 BCE, brought about significant advancements with the discovery and utilization of iron, a stronger and more abundant metal than bronze. This era witnessed profound changes in technology, society, and warfare The Early Iron Age saw the gradual transition from bronze to iron tools and weapons. Ironworking techniques allowed for the production of more durable and efficient tools, enabling further improvements in agriculture, craftsmanship, and warfare. Iron objects became more widely accessible, reducing the socio-economic disparities seen in the Bronze Age.

The La Tène culture, named after an archaeological site in Switzerland, emerged during the Middle Iron Age. This culture was characterized by intricate art styles, such as the famous swirling and curvilinear motifs found in metalwork and jewelry. La Tène communities engaged in extensive trade networks, exchanging goods and ideas across Europe. The Late Iron Age, also known as the Roman Iron Age, was marked by the Roman conquest of Switzerland. The Romans introduced their administrative systems, infrastructure, and cultural practices to the region. This period witnessed the construction of roads, bridges, and towns, leading to urbanization and the integration of Swiss society into the Roman Empire.

Switzerland's archaeological history reveals the significant transitions that occurred during the Stone, Bronze, and Iron Ages. From the nomadic lifestyles of early hunter-gatherers to the settled agricultural communities and advanced metalworking techniques, these eras laid the foundation for the development of Swiss society. The cultural, technological, and social changes that took place during these periods shaped the course of history and provide valuable insights into the lives of ancient Swiss inhabitants.

HELVETIANS & ROMANS

Among Switzerland's earliest inhabitants were the Helvetians, a fascinating ancient people who left an indelible mark on the region. The Helvetians were a Celtic tribe that inhabited what is now modern-day Switzerland during the Iron Age, approximately from the 5th to the 1st century BCE. They were a proud and independent people, known for their bravery and agricultural skills. The Helvetians lived in small, fortified villages nestled in the valleys and mountains of the region, cultivating crops such as wheat, barley, and oats. They also raised livestock, primarily cattle, which played a crucial role in their society and economy.

Helvetian society was organized into clans, led by chieftains who governed their respective communities. These chieftains, chosen based on their wisdom and strength, made important decisions for the tribe. The Helvetians were skilled craftsmen and created intricate jewelry, pottery, and tools. They were known for their impressive metalwork, particularly in bronze and iron. Religion played a significant role in Helvetian culture, and they worshipped a pantheon of gods and goddesses, such as Lug, the god of light, and Belenus, the god of the sun. The Helvetians believed in an afterlife and practiced burial rituals, often burying their deceased with personal belongings.

Driven by a desire for fertile lands and

resources, the Helvetians began to expand their territory. Their migration and conflicts with neighboring tribes brought them into contact with the powerful Roman Republic. In 58 BCE, the Helvetians embarked on a mass migration westward, seeking new lands away from Roman influence. However, their plans were thwarted by the Roman general Julius Caesar, who feared their migration would pose a threat to Rome's interests. Caesar intercepted and defeated the Helvetians, forcing them to return to their homeland. The Helvetians' defeat marked the end of their independence, as they eventually became a part of the Roman province of Gallia Belgica.

Although the Helvetians were assimilated into the Roman Empire, their legacy endured. The name "Helvetia" continued to be associated with the region, eventually becoming the Latin name for Switzerland. Their agricultural practices and craftsmanship skills persisted and influenced subsequent cultures in the region. Today, Switzerland pays tribute to the Helvetians through its national emblem, the Swiss cross, which originates from the Celtic tradition. Helvetian artifacts, including beautifully crafted jewelry and tools, have been discovered throughout Switzerland, shedding light on their advanced civilization.

By 15 BCE, the Romans had established a solid presence in Switzerland. The Romans established numerous settlements, fortifications, and road networks throughout the region. They constructed well-engineered roads, including the Via Augusta, connecting the Roman provinces across the Alps. These roads facilitated trade and communication, boosting economic growth. The Romans also built aqueducts, bridges, and public buildings, showcasing their architectural prowess. These structures served as centers for administration, commerce, and public gatherings. Many of these Roman constructions can still be seen in Switzerland today, reminding us of their lasting impact.

As the Romans settled in Switzerland, they introduced their culture, customs, and language to the local population. Latin, the language of the Romans, became widespread and evolved into the precursor of modern Romance languages, including French, Italian, and Romansh, spoken in Switzerland today. The Romans brought their religious beliefs and practices, constructing temples and shrines dedicated to various deities. They also introduced the concept of public baths, which became social gathering places for the communities. Additionally, Roman-style villas showcased the opulence and refinement of Roman culture.

The Romans' departure from Switzerland in the 5th century CE marked the end of their direct rule. However, their influence remained embedded in the region's history. Roman ruins, such as the amphitheater in Augusta Raurica and the Roman theater in Avenches, continue to attract visitors, providing glimpses into the past. Archaeological excavations have unearthed valuable artifacts and provided insights into Roman life in Switzerland. Museums, such as the Roman Museum in Avenches, preserve these findings and educate visitors about this fascinating era.

The Romans left an indelible mark on Switzerland's history, shaping its culture, infrastructure, and language. Their conquests brought forth advancements in architecture, trade, and governance. The remnants of their presence, including roads, bridges, and ruins, stand as a testament to their enduring legacy. By understanding the Romans' influence, we gain a deeper appreciation of Switzerland's historical tapestry, where the echoes of ancient civilizations still resonate today.

OLD SWISS CONFEDERACY

The roots of the Old Swiss Confederacy can be traced back to the 13th century, a time when Europe was undergoing significant social and political changes. In the heart of the Swiss Alps, small rural communities sought protection against external threats and internal conflicts. Mutual defense agreements known as "eternal leagues" were established, uniting communities to defend their shared interests. The most famous of these leagues were the Three Forest Cantons (Uri, Schwyz, and Unterwalden), which are often regarded as the founding members of the Old Swiss Confederacy.

Over time, other regions and cities joined the confederacy, including Lucerne, Zurich, Bern, and Glarus. The confederacy was characterized by a system of direct democracy, where decisions were made collectively in assemblies called Landsgemeinden. The confederates aimed to preserve their independence and protect their local customs and privileges.

The Old Swiss Confederacy faced numerous challenges. One significant threat came from the Habsburg dynasty, which sought to expand its power over the Swiss territories. The confederates fiercely resisted the Habsburgs in the legendary battles of Morgarten (1315) and Sempach (1386). These victories solidified the confederacy's reputation as a formidable force and bolstered their resolve to maintain their autonomy.

The confederates developed a reputation for their military skills and were often sought after as mercenaries by various European powers. This practice, known as the Swiss mercenary tradition, continued for centuries and brought wealth and prestige to the confederacy. During the 15th century, the confederacy faced internal conflicts between rural and urban cantons, primarily due to economic differences and religious tensions.

The Reformation, spearheaded by figures such as Ulrich Zwingli and later embraced by John Calvin, had a profound impact on Switzerland. The confederacy was divided along religious lines, resulting in the formation of Protestant and Catholic cantons. Despite these divisions, the confederacy maintained its unity and adopted the Treaty of Westphalia in 1648, recognizing Switzerland's independence from the Holy Roman Empire. The Old Swiss Confederacy laid the foundation for modern Switzerland. The confederacy's emphasis on decentralized power, direct democracy, and neutrality shaped the country's political system.

Today, Switzerland continues to be governed by a federal system with strong cantonal autonomy, and decisions are often made through referendums, reflecting the principles of direct democracy. Switzerland's neutrality, which originated during the confederacy, has remained a hallmark of the nation's foreign policy. This neutrality has allowed

Switzerland to maintain a position of peace and avoid involvement in armed conflicts, earning the country international respect and becoming a hub for diplomacy and humanitarian efforts.

The Old Swiss Confederacy stands as a testament to the resilience, unity, and determination of the Swiss people. From humble beginnings, this alliance of independent states grew into a formidable force that shaped Swiss history. The confederacy's values of direct democracy, independence, and neutrality continue to influence Switzerland's political system and foreign policy today. By understanding the legacy of the Old Swiss Confederacy, we gain insights into the roots of Switzerland's unique identity as a nation known for its stability, prosperity, and commitment to peace.

REFORMATION & COUNTERREFORMATION

Switzerland's history is marked by significant religious transformations, particularly during the Reformation and Counter-Reformation periods. The Reformation, led by influential figures like Ulrich Zwingli and John Calvin, challenged the established Roman Catholic Church and sought to reform religious practices. Concurrently, the Counter-Reformation aimed to revitalize Catholicism in response to Protestant movements. In Switzerland, these movements had a profound impact on society, politics, and culture.

The Reformation in Switzerland emerged during the early 16th century, primarily influenced by the ideas of Ulrich Zwingli. Zwingli, a priest in Zurich, criticized the corruption within the Roman Catholic Church, advocating for a return to the simplicity and purity of early Christianity. His teachings gained popularity, leading to significant religious and societal changes. Zwingli's reform efforts focused on scripture-centered worship, rejecting certain traditional practices such as the veneration of saints and the use of images. The formation of the Zurich Consensus in 1523 marked a key milestone, outlining religious reforms and establishing a new church order. Other Swiss cities, such as Basel and Bern, embraced Zwingli's ideas and implemented similar reforms.

The spread of Reformation ideas in Switzerland was not limited to Zwingli's influence alone. John Calvin, a French theologian, found refuge in Geneva, where he shaped the city's religious and social fabric. Calvin's teachings emphasized predestination, the authority of scripture, and a strict moral code. Geneva became a significant center for Reformed Protestantism, attracting followers and scholars from across Europe.

The Reformation movement faced opposition from Catholic authorities and conservative factions. This led to conflicts between the Catholic and Protestant cantons, most notably the Kappel Wars, fought in 1529 and 1531. These conflicts resulted in a compromise known as the First Peace of Kappel, allowing each canton to determine its own religion. The peace was short-lived, as tensions continued to simmer, leading to the Second Peace of Kappel in 1531, which solidified the division between Catholic and Protestant cantons.

In response to the Protestant Reformation, the Roman Catholic Church initiated the Counter-Reformation, aiming to address the causes of the Reformation and win back converts. The Council of Trent (1545-1563) played a central role in defining Catholic doctrine and implementing reforms. Switzerland, being a predominantly Protestant region, saw concerted efforts by Catholic authorities to reassert their influence. The Society of Jesus, founded by Ignatius of Loyola in 1540, played a crucial role in the Counter-Reformation. Jesuit missionaries arrived in Switzerland to promote Catholic teachings, establish schools, and engage in intellectual debates. Their presence contributed to a revival of Catholicism in some regions, particularly in the cantons of Lucerne and Fribourg.

Additionally, the Ursuline Order, a female religious order, opened schools and focused on the education of girls, offering an alternative to Protestant educational institutions. These efforts aimed to counter the influence of Protestant teachings and ensure the preservation of Catholic traditions. The Swiss Catholic Church implemented internal reforms, including the establishment of seminaries for the education of priests, stricter discipline, and improved pastoral care. The Catholic cantons also collaborated in the creation of the Golden Apples, a league formed to defend Catholic interests and promote unity among Catholic territories.

The Reformation and Counter-Reformation had lasting impacts on Switzerland's history and cultural identity. The Reformation challenged the authority of the Catholic Church and brought about religious pluralism in Switzerland. The division between Protestant and Catholic cantons created a distinctive religious landscape, with each canton having the autonomy to govern its religious affairs.

The Reformation also fostered the development of an educated society. Protestant reformers emphasized the importance of literacy, resulting in the establishment of schools and universities. This emphasis on education contributed to Switzerland's reputation as a center of intellectual and academic excellence.

The Counter-Reformation, while not achieving the complete restoration of Catholicism, managed to reinvigorate Catholic communities in certain regions. The educational institutions established by Catholic orders left a lasting legacy in Swiss education and culture. The religious divisions during the Reformation period also had political implications. The conflicts between Protestant and Catholic cantons laid the groundwork for Switzerland's unique system of federalism, with different regions having distinct religious and political identities.

The Reformation and Counter-Reformation periods in Switzerland's history were transformative and shaped the country's religious, cultural, and political landscape. The ideas and reforms introduced by reformers like Zwingli and Calvin, as well as the response of the Catholic Church, continue to influence Swiss society to this day. Understanding this pivotal era helps us appreciate the diversity and complexity of Switzerland's historical tapestry.

SWISS REVOLUTION & FEDERAL STATEHOOD

The Swiss Revolution stands as a pivotal event in the history of Switzerland. It took place in the late 18th century and brought significant changes to the country's political landscape. This revolution was driven by a desire for greater freedom, equality, and democratic governance. While it may not be as well-known as other revolutions, its impact on Switzerland's development cannot be underestimated.

Prior to the Swiss Revolution, Switzerland was a confederation of independent states, each with its own laws and rulers. The country was marked by social inequality and limited political rights for the common people. The revolution gained momentum in the late 18th century, inspired by the ideas of the Enlightenment and the success of the American and French revolutions. Several factors contributed to the outbreak of the Swiss Revolution. The widespread discontent among the Swiss population was fueled by economic hardships, social inequality, and political oppression. The ideas of equality, individual rights, and sovereignty propagated by Enlightenment philosophers also played a crucial role in stirring up revolutionary sentiment.

The Swiss Revolution began with protests and demands for political reform. In 1798, French troops invaded Switzerland, quickly defeating the ruling powers and establishing the Helvetic Republic. The new government aimed to centralize power, abolish feudalism, and introduce equal rights for all citizens. However, these changes faced resistance from conservative forces who sought to preserve the old order. Although the Helvetic Republic ultimately failed, the revolution paved the way for the establishment of the Swiss Confederation in 1848, which laid the foundation for the modern Swiss state.

The revolution led to the creation of a new constitution, which introduced democratic principles and guaranteed individual rights. One of the most significant legacies of the Swiss Revolution was the notion of Swiss neutrality. During the upheaval, Switzerland managed to remain relatively unscathed by the Napoleonic Wars, which engulfed Europe during that time. This period of neutrality allowed Switzerland to develop into a prosperous and stable nation. The Swiss Revolution marked a turning point in Switzerland's history, as it set the stage for the establishment of a more democratic and egalitarian society. The revolution's influence can still be felt in modern-day Switzerland, where political power rests with the people and individual rights are protected.

Central to Switzerland's governance is the concept of federal statehood, which has played a pivotal role in shaping the nation's history. The roots of Switzerland's federal statehood can be traced back to the Middle Ages, when various regions within the country banded together for mutual protection and economic cooperation. These alliances, known as "cantons," gradually formed the foundation of Switzerland's political system. The earliest known document outlining the principles of federal statehood is the Federal Charter of 1291. This charter established the union of three cantons: Uri, Schwyz, and Unterwalden.

As Switzerland expanded, additional cantons were admitted to the confederation, leading to the establishment of a federal government. In 1848, the modern Swiss federal state was officially created with the adoption of a new constitution. This constitution emphasized the importance of individual freedoms, equality, and the separation of powers. It also outlined the division of responsibilities between the federal government and the cantons, ensuring a balance of power and local autonomy.

Under the federal system, Switzerland's government consists of three branches: the executive, legislative, and judicial. The executive branch, known as the Federal Council, is composed of seven members who are elected by the Federal Assembly. The legislative branch, comprising two chambers— the National Council and the Council of States— passes laws and represents the interests of the cantons and citizens. The judicial branch, through the Federal Supreme Court, ensures the application of laws and the protection of individual rights.

Federal statehood in Switzerland offers several advantages that have contributed to the nation's stability and prosperity. Firstly, it allows for a distribution of power between the central government and the cantons, ensuring that decisions are made at the appropriate level. This decentralized structure accommodates Switzerland's linguistic, cultural, and geographical diversity, enabling individual cantons to address local needs effectively. Additionally, federal statehood promotes political stability through power-sharing and consensus-building mechanisms. The Swiss federal government operates on a consensual basis, with decisions often requiring broad agreement among different cantons and political parties. This system encourages cooperation, compromise, and the representation of diverse viewpoints.

Switzerland's federal statehood has been instrumental in shaping the nation's history, promoting stability, and accommodating its diverse population. From its humble beginnings as a union of three cantons, the Swiss Confederation has evolved into a thriving federal state with a robust political system. By recognizing the importance of local autonomy, power-sharing, and consensus-building, Switzerland has achieved political harmony and ensured the well-being of its citizens for centuries—a testament to the enduring success of federal statehood in Switzerland.

INDUSTRIALIZATION & INFRASTRUCTURE

Switzerland is known for its history of industrialization and infrastructure development. For much of its history, Switzerland was primarily an agrarian society. The country's rugged terrain and abundant natural resources provided a solid foundation for agriculture. Farms were scattered across the countryside, and local craftsmen catered to the basic needs of communities. The absence of large-scale industries, however, limited economic growth and progress.

The seeds of industrialization were sown in Switzerland during the late 18th century. The country embraced the emerging textile industry, which spurred urbanization and transformed the economy. The textile mills of Zurich and St. Gallen became bustling centers of production, attracting workers from rural areas. Engineers played a crucial role in connecting regions, harnessing natural resources, and modernizing transportation networks. The Swiss quickly realized the importance of efficient transportation, and significant efforts were made to construct an extensive railway system. The first railway line, connecting Zurich and Baden, was inaugurated in 1847, marking the dawn of a new era.

The construction of railways facilitated the movement of goods and people across the country.

Notably, the Gotthard Railway, a monumental engineering feat completed in 1882, connected northern and southern Switzerland through the treacherous Alps. This achievement further strengthened Switzerland's position as a trade hub and accelerated economic growth. Switzerland's abundant water resources played a pivotal role in its industrialization and electrification. The harnessing of hydropower became a key priority, allowing the establishment of power plants to supply electricity for industrial processes. The pioneering efforts of engineers and entrepreneurs led to the development of hydroelectric power plants in various regions, such as the Rhine Falls Power Plant in Schaffhausen.

Switzerland's commitment to infrastructure development did not wane in the 20th century. The construction of highways, tunnels, and bridges became paramount, allowing for seamless connectivity between cities and regions. Notably, the Swiss developed an intricate network of tunnels, including the renowned Gotthard Base Tunnel, the longest railway tunnel in the world. These infrastructure investments not only enhanced transportation but also provided a solid foundation for continued economic growth and technological innovation.

Switzerland's history of industrialization and infrastructure development is a testament to the nation's determination, ingenuity, and commitment to progress. From its agrarian roots to the cutting-edge industries of today, Switzerland's journey has been marked by remarkable achievements in engineering, transportation, and power generation. The country's focus on innovation and infrastructure has contributed to its global reputation for precision engineering, high-quality manufacturing, and economic stability.

WORLD WARS I & 2

    Switzerland's history is intertwined with the two most significant conflicts of the 20th century: World War I and World War II. While Switzerland maintained its neutrality during both wars, its strategic position and policies significantly impacted its citizens and its relationship with the belligerent nations. Surrounded by warring nations, including Germany, France, and Austria-Hungary, Switzerland's geographical position shielded it from direct military conflicts. The country's neutral stance, backed by a strong militia and fortified borders, deterred any potential aggressors.

    While Switzerland escaped the direct horrors of the battlefields, it faced significant economic challenges during World War I. The blockade of goods and resources impacted trade, causing shortages and price inflation. As the conflict raged on, Switzerland faced a substantial influx of refugees from neighboring countries. Displaced civilians, fleeing persecution and violence, sought safety within the Swiss borders. The Swiss government, recognizing its humanitarian duty, established internment camps and provided assistance to the refugees. Though not without challenges, Switzerland managed to accommodate hundreds of thousands of individuals, including intellectuals, artists, and political dissidents.

    As tensions escalated prior to World War II,

Switzerland faced immense political pressure from Nazi Germany. Adolf Hitler's regime sought to infiltrate Switzerland's financial system, control strategic routes, and exploit Swiss resources. The Swiss government and its citizens resisted these attempts, navigating a delicate diplomatic dance to maintain their neutrality. Switzerland bolstered its defense mechanisms to protect its sovereignty. The Swiss Army mobilized its forces, fortified its borders, and prepared for a potential invasion. The Swiss people, trained in militia service, provided a formidable defense, dissuading any aggressor from considering an attack.

Switzerland faced another significant refugee crisis during World War II. As Hitler's regime unleashed its persecution against Jews and other targeted groups, Switzerland became a beacon of hope for those seeking refuge. The Swiss government, facing internal divisions and pressure from neighboring countries, adopted stricter refugee policies. Despite the challenges, Switzerland provided asylum to a significant number of individuals, saving countless lives. After the conclusion of World War II, Switzerland faced the task of rebuilding and reconciling with neighboring countries. Despite the devastation suffered by Europe, Switzerland experienced rapid economic recovery and emerged as a prosperous nation.

Switzerland's unique position during World War I and World War II as a neutral nation provided both challenges and opportunities. The country's geographical location, economic resilience, and humanitarian efforts contributed to its ability to maintain neutrality despite intense external pressures. Switzerland's experiences during these global conflicts shaped its identity as a nation committed to neutrality, humanitarian values, and international cooperation. By examining Switzerland's history during the World Wars, we gain insight into the complexities of war and the crucial role played by neutral nations in preserving peace and providing refuge in times of crisis.

POST WAR PROSPERITY

After the devastating conflicts of World War II came to an end, many nations around the world faced the arduous task of rebuilding their economies and societies. Switzerland was one such country that experienced a remarkable post-war transformation. As the war concluded in 1945, Switzerland faced several challenges on its path to recovery. Despite its neutrality, the country had to overcome economic hardships, shortages, and a significant influx of refugees. However, Switzerland's long-standing traditions of stability, innovation, and a skilled workforce laid the foundation for its post-war resurgence.

Switzerland's pre-war economic stability played a crucial role in its post-war success. The nation possessed a robust banking system, a strong currency, and a tradition of fiscal discipline. These factors helped Switzerland recover swiftly and establish itself as a major economic force. Switzerland's commitment to education and research was a key driver of its post-war prosperity. Recognizing the importance of an educated workforce, the Swiss government invested heavily in schools, universities, and vocational training programs. This emphasis on education and skills development provided the nation with a highly skilled labor force, attracting both domestic and foreign investment.

Switzerland's renowned banking and financial sector played a significant role in the nation's post-war prosperity. The country's neutrality during the war, coupled with its strong banking secrecy laws, made it an attractive destination for international funds seeking a safe haven. Swiss banks thrived as they offered stability, confidentiality, and expertise to investors worldwide, further strengthening Switzerland's economic position. Switzerland's post-war era witnessed substantial investments in infrastructure development. The country improved its transportation network, including roads, railways, and airports, facilitating trade and connectivity within and beyond its borders.

The post-war period saw an increase in tourism, as people sought peace, tranquility, and natural beauty. Furthermore, Switzerland's tradition of neutrality and diplomacy helped establish strong international relations, enabling favorable trade agreements and partnerships that contributed to its economic growth. Switzerland's post-war prosperity was not solely measured in economic terms; it also encompassed improvements in social welfare and the overall quality of life for its citizens. The Swiss government implemented policies that focused on providing universal healthcare, affordable housing, and a strong social safety net. These measures helped foster social cohesion and stability within the country.

Switzerland's remarkable post-war prosperity can be attributed to a combination of factors, including economic stability, investment in education and research, a thriving banking sector, infrastructure development, and the promotion of tourism and international relations. By leveraging its strengths and embracing innovation, Switzerland emerged as a model of economic success and social progress. The legacy of post-war prosperity continues to shape Switzerland's position as a prosperous and forward-thinking nation.

HISTORICAL PLACES

Located in Avenches, the Roman Aventicum stands as a testament to Switzerland's Roman heritage. Founded over 2,000 years ago, Aventicum was once the capital of the Helvetians, a Celtic tribe. It flourished under Roman rule and became an important administrative and cultural center. Today, visitors can explore the well-preserved ruins of the Roman theater, the amphitheater, and the thermal baths, which offer a glimpse into the everyday life of ancient Romans. The archaeological museum nearby exhibits a collection of artifacts from the Roman era, shedding light on Aventicum's historical significance.

Situated on the shores of Lake Geneva near Montreux, Chillon Castle is a medieval fortress that has captivated visitors for centuries. With its imposing towers and picturesque location, the castle is steeped in legends and tales of medieval times. Built in the 12th century, Chillon Castle served as a strategic stronghold and a residence for the Counts of Savoy. Visitors can wander through its labyrinthine halls, admire the magnificent frescoes, and explore the underground chambers where prisoners were once held captive. The castle's long history and stunning architecture make it a must-visit destination.

The Abbey of St. Gall, located in the city of St. Gallen, is a UNESCO World Heritage site and a symbol of Switzerland's religious and cultural heritage. Founded in the 8th century, the abbey played a crucial role in the spread of Christianity in Europe. The abbey's library is renowned for its vast collection of medieval manuscripts, including the famous St. Gallen manuscripts, which provide invaluable insights into medieval life and culture. The abbey's Baroque cathedral, with its ornate interior and stunning rococo-style library hall, is a masterpiece of architectural and artistic brilliance.

Nestled in the city of Lucerne, the Wooden Bridge Chapel, or the Chapel Bridge (Kapellbrücke), is not only a picturesque landmark but also an important historical site. Dating back to the 14th century, this covered wooden bridge is Europe's oldest surviving truss bridge. Adorned with vibrant paintings depicting scenes from Swiss history and mythology, the bridge offers visitors a fascinating journey through time. Tragically, the bridge was partially destroyed by a fire in 1993, but it was meticulously reconstructed, preserving its historical charm.

Located in Geneva, the Cathedral of St. Pierre is an iconic symbol of the city's religious and historical heritage. Dating back to the 12th century, this majestic cathedral is renowned for its stunning architectural features, including a mix of Gothic and Romanesque styles. Climb the tower's 157 steps for breathtaking panoramic views of Geneva and the surrounding area. The cathedral also holds historical significance as it served as a center for the Protestant Reformation in the 16th century, with influential reformer John Calvin preaching within its walls.

Historical People

One of Switzerland's most iconic figures, William Tell, has come to symbolize the Swiss struggle for independence and liberty. According to legend, Tell was an expert marksman who defied the tyrannical rule of the Austrian Habsburgs in the early 14th century. He is famously known for shooting an apple off his son's head, an act that demonstrated his unwavering commitment to freedom. While the historical accuracy of the Tell legend is debated, his story has become a powerful symbol of Swiss nationalism and resistance against oppression.

Jean-Jacques Rousseau, a philosopher and writer, was born in Geneva and became one of the most influential thinkers of the Enlightenment era. His works, such as "The Social Contract" and "Emile," laid the foundations for modern political and educational theories. Rousseau's ideas on the social contract, individual freedom, and the importance of education influenced the development of democracy and liberalism not only in Switzerland but also around the world. His intellectual legacy continues to shape political and philosophical discourse to this day.

Henri Dunant, a Swiss businessman and social activist, is the founder of the International Committee of the Red Cross (ICRC). After witnessing the horrific aftermath of the Battle of Solferino in 1859, Dunant was moved by the suffering of wounded soldiers and civilians. His experiences led him to establish the ICRC, an organization dedicated to providing medical aid, protection, and relief to victims of armed conflicts and disasters. Dunant's humanitarian efforts resulted in the creation of the Geneva Conventions, which laid the groundwork for international humanitarian law and the protection of human rights.

While Albert Einstein was born in Germany, his contributions to science and his association with Switzerland make him an integral part of Swiss history. Einstein, a physicist best known for his theory of relativity, spent several pivotal years in Switzerland, where he obtained his education and developed groundbreaking ideas. In 1905, Einstein published his special theory of relativity, revolutionizing our understanding of space, time, and energy. His genius and scientific achievements earned him the Nobel Prize in Physics in 1921. Einstein's work continues to shape our understanding of the universe and remains a source of inspiration for scientists worldwide.

Charles-Édouard Jeanneret, known by his pseudonym Le Corbusier, was a Swiss-French architect, designer, and urban planner. Considered one of the pioneers of modern architecture, Le Corbusier's innovative ideas transformed the way we think about urban spaces and housing. His principles of functionalism, open floor plans, and the use of reinforced concrete revolutionized architectural design. Le Corbusier's iconic works, such as the Villa Savoye and the Unité d'Habitation, continue to inspire architects and shape urban landscapes around the world.

Hist**o**rical F**oo**ds

One of the most famous foods from Switzerland is the Swiss dish of fondue. Fondue, derived from the French word "fondre" meaning "to melt," has a history dating back to the late 17th century. Initially born out of necessity, this communal dish gained popularity in the Swiss Alps, where people used melted cheese to make stale bread more palatable during the long winters.

Fondue's modern incarnation consists of a blend of Swiss cheeses such as Gruyère and Emmental, melted together with white wine and garlic. Traditionally, a communal pot called a "caquelon" is used, and diners dip pieces of bread into the molten cheese using long forks. The convivial nature of fondue has made it a social dining experience enjoyed by Swiss families and visitors alike.

Another cheese-based delight hailing from the Swiss Alps is raclette. Originating in the canton of Valais, raclette has a history that can be traced back several centuries. Historically, shepherds would melt cheese by the fire and scrape it onto bread or potatoes, creating a simple yet satisfying meal.

Raclette cheese, typically made from cow's milk, is melted and served with boiled potatoes, pickles, and onions. The name "raclette" comes from the French word "racler," meaning "to scrape," referring to the act of scraping the melted cheese onto the accompaniments. Today, raclette has become a cherished Swiss specialty, enjoyed in restaurants and homes across the country.

Moving away from cheese, let's explore a traditional Swiss potato dish called rösti. This hearty culinary creation is believed to have originated as a farmer's breakfast in the Bern region during the 19th century. Rösti was a way for farmers to use up leftover boiled potatoes, which were grated, fried, and seasoned with salt and pepper.

Rösti gained popularity and evolved into a versatile dish served throughout Switzerland. Today, it is typically prepared by frying grated potatoes in a pan until golden and crispy. Rösti is often enjoyed as a side dish accompanying various meat dishes or as a standalone main course, sometimes topped with eggs, cheese, or vegetables.

For those with a taste for meat, Zürcher Geschnetzeltes offers a delectable option. This dish originated in Zurich and has become one of Switzerland's most famous culinary exports. It consists of thinly sliced veal cooked in a creamy white wine and mushroom sauce, served with Rösti.

The origins of Zürcher Geschnetzeltes can be traced back to the 19th century when the Swiss military adopted French cooking techniques. The soldiers brought the recipe back to Zurich, where it gained popularity and became a staple of Swiss cuisine. Today, this savory dish can be found in many Swiss restaurants, delighting locals and tourists alike.

No exploration of Swiss cuisine would be complete without mentioning its world-renowned chocolate. Switzerland's love affair with chocolate began in the early 19th century when François-Louis Cailler established the country's first chocolate factory in Corsier-sur-Vevey.

Since then, Swiss chocolate has become synonymous with quality and craftsmanship. Renowned for its smooth texture and rich flavors, Swiss chocolate is made from high-quality cocoa beans and blended with milk or cream. Chocolatiers across Switzerland create an array of mouthwatering chocolate treats, from milk chocolate bars to pralines, truffles, and more.

Swiss Alps

The Swiss Alps, a majestic mountain range located in the heart of Europe, have captivated the imagination of people for centuries. With their snow-capped peaks, pristine glaciers, and lush valleys, they are not only a breathtaking natural wonder but also an essential part of Switzerland's rich heritage. Let us delve into the history of the Swiss Alps, exploring their geological formation, early human settlements, cultural significance, and economic impact.

The story of the Swiss Alps begins millions of years ago during the formation of the Earth's crust. These mountains were shaped through the collision of tectonic plates, specifically the Eurasian and African plates. The immense pressure caused the Earth's crust to buckle and fold, creating the towering peaks we see today. Glaciers also played a crucial role in shaping the landscape. During the Ice Age, massive glaciers sculpted the valleys and carved out deep gorges, leaving behind picturesque lakes.

The Swiss Alps have been inhabited since prehistoric times. The first evidence of human presence in the region dates back to the Paleolithic era, around 10,000 BCE. Early hunter-gatherer societies roamed the Alps, utilizing the available resources for survival. Over time, Neolithic communities settled in the valleys, engaging in agriculture and animal husbandry. These early settlers, known as the Alpine Celts, established trade routes and developed a distinct culture.

During the Roman period, from the 1st century BCE to the 5th century CE, the Romans conquered the region and left their mark on the Alps. They built roads, such as the Via Augusta, which connected Italy with the northern territories. The Romans also established towns and mining operations, exploiting the rich mineral resources of the Alps.

The Swiss Alps have played a significant role in shaping the culture and identity of Switzerland. The mountainous terrain has historically provided a natural defense, enabling the development of independent communities. The concept of federalism, the idea of decentralized governance, emerged in Switzerland as a response to the challenging geography.

Religion has also been closely intertwined with the Alps. In the Middle Ages, Christian monasteries were established in the mountains, offering refuge and spreading religious teachings. The most renowned of these monasteries is the Great St. Bernard Hospice, located on the pass of the same name, which has provided shelter to travelers and pilgrims for centuries.

The Alps have also inspired countless artists, writers, and musicians. From the romantic paintings of Caspar David Friedrich to the enchanting melodies of classical composer Ludwig van Beethoven, the Swiss Alps have served as a muse for creativity and expression.

The Swiss Alps have long been an important economic resource for the region. Historically, agriculture and animal husbandry have been the primary livelihoods for mountain dwellers. Farmers cultivated terraced fields, raised livestock, and produced dairy products, such as cheese and butter. The unique Alpine flora and fauna have contributed to the distinct taste and quality of Swiss products.

In the 19th century, the development of tourism began to transform the Alpine region. Travelers from around the world were drawn to the natural beauty and charm of the mountains. Swiss hotels and resorts sprang up, catering to the growing demand for leisure activities like skiing, hiking, and mountaineering. Today, tourism remains a vital source of income for many Alpine communities.

Today, the Swiss Alps continue to enchant visitors with their awe-inspiring landscapes, offering a myriad of outdoor activities and breathtaking vistas. As we marvel at the snow-capped peaks and explore the quaint villages nestled in the valleys, let us remember the rich history that has shaped this remarkable mountain range and its enduring impact on Switzerland and the world.

SWISS SPORTS

Football, or soccer, holds a special place in the hearts of Swiss sports fans. The Swiss Football Association (SFV) is responsible for organizing and governing football activities in the country. Switzerland boasts a vibrant football scene with both professional and amateur leagues. The Swiss Super League, the top-tier football league in Switzerland, features exciting matches between renowned clubs like FC Basel, FC Zurich, and Young Boys. The national team, known as the "Nati," garners immense support during international tournaments such as the FIFA World Cup and the UEFA European Championship.

Ice hockey is a thrilling sport enjoyed by many Swiss citizens. The Swiss National League (NL) serves as the pinnacle of professional ice hockey in Switzerland, showcasing high-level competition among teams like HC Davos, SC Bern, and ZSC Lions. The Swiss ice hockey team, often referred to as the "Ice Hockey Nati," has participated in numerous international tournaments, including the Winter Olympics and the Ice Hockey World Championships. The speed, physicality, and strategic gameplay of ice hockey make it a beloved sport in Switzerland.

With its breathtaking mountains and snowy slopes, it's no surprise that alpine skiing is immensely popular in Switzerland. This winter sport involves gliding down the mountainside on skis. Switzerland has numerous world-class ski resorts, including Zermatt, St. Moritz, and Verbier, which attract skiing enthusiasts from around the globe. Swiss skiers have achieved great success in international competitions, such as the FIS Alpine Ski World Cup, the Winter Olympics, and the World Championships, solidifying Switzerland's reputation as a powerhouse in alpine skiing.

Tennis enjoys a dedicated following in Switzerland, thanks in large part to the country's most successful tennis player, Roger Federer. Federer, a global icon and one of the greatest tennis players of all time, has inspired generations of Swiss tennis enthusiasts. The Swiss Indoors Basel, an ATP World Tour 500 series event held in Basel, is a major highlight of the Swiss tennis calendar. The tournament attracts top-ranked players, showcasing the country's passion for the sport. Additionally, Switzerland's Fed Cup and Davis Cup teams have achieved notable success on the international stage.

Cycling has gained significant popularity in Switzerland, both as a recreational activity and as a competitive sport. The Swiss landscape, with its stunning mountain passes and picturesque cycling routes, provides an ideal setting for cyclists of all levels. The Tour de Suisse takes place annually in Switzerland. Swiss cyclists, such as Fabian Cancellara and Stefan Küng, have excelled in road cycling, while the country's mountain biking scene attracts riders eager to conquer the challenging trails.

WELCOME TO SWITZERLAND!

KID PLANET BOOKS ARE WRITTEN TO HELP CHILDREN LEARN!

KID PLANET BOOKS

LOGAN STOVER IS AN AUTHOR, HISTORIAN, & THE CREATOR OF KID PLANET CHILDREN'S BOOKS!

"LOGAN HAS A GIFT FOR TEACHING HISTORY AND MAKES LEARNING FUN!"

www.KIDPLANETBOOKS.com
www.LOGANSTOVER.com

Made in the USA
Las Vegas, NV
26 November 2024